Job Strategies for New Employees

Robert W. Lucas

American Media Publishing
4900 University Avenue
West Des Moines, IA 50266-6769
800-262-2557

2/03

Job Strategies for New Employees

Robert W. Lucas
Copyright ©1996 by Robert W. Lucas

This publication is designed to provide accurate and authoritative information in regard to the subject matter covered. It is sold with the understanding that neither the author nor the publisher is engaged in rendering legal, accounting, or other professional service. If legal advice or other expert assistance is required, the services of a competent professional should be sought.

Credits:

American Media Publishing:	Arthur Bauer
	Todd McDonald
	Esther Vanier
Managing Editor:	Karen Massetti Miller
Designer:	Gayle O'Brien
Cover Design:	Polly Beaver

Published by American Media Inc.
4900 University Avenue
West Des Moines, IA 50266-6769

Library of Congress Catalog Card Number 96-84913
Lucus, Robert W.
Job Strategies for New Employees

Printed in the United States of America
1997
ISBN 1-884926-55-X

Introduction

For more than 24 years, I have worked with employees at all levels in organizations. During this period, I have held a number of frontline and management jobs and have been employed as an internal and external consultant in a variety of workplace environments—military, government, profit, nonprofit, and volunteer. This diverse background has given me some unique insights as an employee, manager, and trainer. In particular, I understand the challenges faced by new employees joining an organization or moving into a new position, department, or team. The Number 1 issue faced by someone in that position, in any organization, is how to communicate and effectively interact with others. As you read through this book, please take the time to stop and reflect periodically upon how you might apply the practical tips offered. Think also of situations you have seen, heard of, or experienced in which you or others new to a job encountered obstacles. Ask yourself these questions:

◆ What were the obstacles?

◆ What was done to overcome them?

◆ What were the results?

◆ Could anything have been done differently to positively influence the outcome(s)?

This book will provide answers to questions you have about entering a new job situation. It will do so through the following format:

◆ Strategies for Success are spread throughout the book.

◆ Chapter objectives will define what you will learn.

◆ Examples of potential job situations encountered in a new position or job will be presented.

◆ Practical, step-by-step solutions to common obstacles will be suggested.

◆ Reviews of key chapter information will be available at the end of chapters.

By applying what you find in this book to your own situation, being open to suggestions for improvement, and continually upgrading your knowledge and skills, you'll be on your way to career success.

About the Author

Robert W. (Bob) Lucas is the Manager of Professional Development at the national office of the American Automobile Association. He is also president of Creative Presentation Resources and Bob Lucas & Associates. He has extensive experience in the training and development, human resources, and management fields. For the past 24 years, Bob has conducted training in a wide variety of organizational environments. His areas of expertise include management and training program development, customer service, interpersonal communication, adult learning, and employee and organizational development.

Bob regularly gives presentations to various local and national groups and organizations and is an adjunct faculty member at several universities. Additionally, Bob has been the president of the Central Florida Chapter of the American Society for Training and Development.

Books Bob has written include *Coaching Skills: A Guide for Supervisors, Effective Interpersonal Relationships, Training Skills for Supervisors,* and *Customer Service: Skills and Concepts for Business.* Additionally, Bob is a contributing author for the 1992, 1994, 1995, and 1996 *Annual: Developing Human Resources* and has published articles for numerous publications.

Bob holds a Bachelor of Science degree from the University of Maryland and a Master of Arts degree with a focus in Human Resource Management from George Mason University in Fairfax, Virginia.

● Table of Contents

Chapter One
Taking Advantage of a New Situation   8

What Can I Expect?   10
What Are My Roles?   12
Using a Mentor to Help You Succeed in Your New Job   19
Chapter Summary   22
Self-Check: Chapter 1 Review   23

Chapter Two
Fitting In and Building Your Network   24

What Is a Network?   24
Building Networking Skills   26
Getting People to Trust You   29
Attributes of an Effective Team Player   30
Gaining Cooperation   33
Chapter Summary   36
Self-Check: Chapter 2 Review   37

Chapter Three
Communicating in Your New Role and Beyond   38

Communicating Effectively   39
The Art of Questioning   41
Avoiding Communication Turn-Offs   45
Listening for Success   46
Recognizing Poor Listening   47
Chapter Summary   48
Self-Check: Chapter 3 Review   49

Chapter Four
Preparing for the Unexpected   50

Why Things Go Wrong   50
Playing "What If . . ."   51
Chapter Summary   60
Self-Check: Chapter 4 Review   61

Chapter Five

Beyond Orientation

Beyond Orientation   **62**

Your Supervisor's Responsibility   63
Possible Questions for Your Supervisor   64
Your Responsibilities   65
Setting Personal Goals   69
Positive Reinforcement   70
Developing the Attitude to Succeed   71
Chapter Summary   74
What's Next   74

Answers to Selected Exercises   **76**

Additional Resources   **79**

Chapter *One*

Taking Advantage of a New Situation

Chapter Objectives

▶ Define your job-related roles more effectively.

▶ Reduce the stress caused by being in a new environment through better mental preparation.

▶ Prepare a list of questions to ask your new supervisor/team leader.

▶ Identify people who can effectively provide mentoring and share knowledge.

Excitement, fear, apprehension, stress, anticipation, ambiguity, self-satisfaction, confidence, insecurity—these are all feelings you may experience moving into a new job, department, team, or organization. Depending on your age, level of experience, time in the job market, knowledge, self-esteem level, and a number of other factors, you may experience some or all of these feelings. The important thing to remember, though, is that someone had confidence in your ability, or you wouldn't be there in the first place.

Additionally, all new job environments are different due to such factors as location, people, job responsibilities, and expectations. Look at your new job as an opportunity to grow professionally and proceed accordingly.

Getting the Information You Need

Before starting your new job, take time to write down questions you have for your supervisor, team leader, and/or orientation leader that were not answered in the interview process. At a minimum, ask:

- What is the organizational/work-unit mission?
- Whom can/should I contact for assistance, if needed?
- What products/services does the organization/work-unit provide?
- Who is/are our customer(s)? (both internal and external)
- What policies/procedures should I be familiar with?
- What are my job responsibilities?
- What is my relationship to other employees/department staff members?
- What are potential problem areas, and how can I avoid them?
- What are your expectations?
- Will I have written performance goals, and how will they be measured? (Ask for an explanation of the performance appraisal process, if applicable.)
- What are my work/holiday/pay schedules?
- What paperwork/reports do I deal with?
- Are there safety/emergency procedures of which I should be aware?

Other questions: _____

_____

_____

_____

Once you arrive at your new job, schedule time to sit down with the appropriate person(s) to discuss your list of questions.

What Can I Expect?

Most organizations and supervisors introduce new employees to their jobs through a process known as *orientation*. Depending on whether you're joining a new organization or just a new department or team within your current organization, this process can be formal (classroom instruction, often handled by the human resource staff) or informal (on-the-job conducted by your supervisor and/or a peer coach).

Generally, formal orientations are broader in scope and address such things as organizational policies/procedures, history, structure, and benefits. Informal orientations often include information on your work-unit culture; departmental/team policies and procedures; job responsibilities; tours of crucial areas; introductions to peers, vendors, and customers; and issues pertinent to your job success.

In the next section, we're going to talk about expectations. Before we do, take a moment to put yourself in your supervisor's shoes.

> **Most organizations and supervisors introduce new employees to their jobs through a process known as *orientation*.**

Take a Moment

Imagine for a minute that you are your new supervisor and that a new employee will be starting work tomorrow. Answer these questions.

What type of behavior will you expect related to attendance/punctuality? _____

What standard of dress will you require for the job?

_____

What level of participation will you expect related to suggestions or change?

_____

How will you expect the employee to act in relation to others?

_____

What level of job knowledge do you expect?

_____

What degree of initiative is expected?

_____

What kind of "attitude" is acceptable?

_____

To what degree will you expect the employee to participate in personal goal setting?

_____

With these questions and responses in mind, read the next section and see how you can better prepare to meet your own described expectations. Your supervisor may be asking these types of questions and more. Being prepared may impress them.

What Are My Roles?

First impressions
are lasting and
can impact your
ultimate level of
success in your
new position.

Your supervisor should explain your formal role(s); however, no matter what job you are starting, you will always be expected to handle some additional responsibilities. Even though these responsibilities may be unwritten or unspoken, you will be held accountable for meeting them. The following are typical in both hierarchal and team environments.

Be Punctual

Arriving at work and returning from breaks and lunch as scheduled is important. You are paid to be at your job during specific time frames. If you are not there, your productivity falls, others may have to pick up your workload (causing resentment toward you), and you are cheating your employer, who pays you for the scheduled hours worked. Early arrival is especially important during your initial period on the job since others are watching and evaluating you. First impressions are lasting and can impact your ultimate level of success in your new position.

Strategies for Success

Develop a system for getting to work before the expected time to compensate for any unforeseen events (traffic jams, accidents, car problems, baby-sitter delays). During your probation period, your supervisor will likely be watching attendance closely, and you should not disappoint him or her. Arriving early also gives you an opportunity to get to know and network with other employees. Usually, these early-arrivals will be the more motivated and enthusiastic employees of the department and can serve as good role models and resources for you.

Project a Professional Appearance

The way you present yourself is crucial to career success. This includes the clothes you wear and making sure that they are cleaned and pressed. Likewise, always practice good personal hygiene. Use moderation with jewelry, makeup, and hair styles (also, facial hair for men). Some styles, practices, and accessories are fine for nonbusiness settings, but they can send the wrong message to supervisors, customers, and coworkers. Since each organization and work-unit has its own culture and practices based on mission/goals, you should look to your supervisor for guidance on what is acceptable.

1

Strategies for Success

Take the time to find out what the dress and grooming standards are while in your employment interview. You should try to comply with standards, otherwise you may be viewed as a rebel or nonconformist from the very beginning and will likely remain an outsider. This will obviously hinder your success.

Comply with Office Etiquette

Being considerate of others and following established protocol will definitely get you off on the right foot. It is not advisable to start your new job trying to "rock the boat" or force change. Even though you may not agree with policies, procedures, or practices in place, take some time to observe quietly before making recommendations for change. Remember that while a practice or procedure may have worked in another place, this is a new job environment, and there may be a reason why certain things are done as they are. Failure to comply with norms can label you as a troublemaker or nonteam player and could lead to problems. Later, if you find you cannot abide by the system in place, and your suggestions for change go unheeded, you may have to admit you are in the wrong job or organization.

Take some time to observe quietly before making recommendations for change.

Strategies for Success

If you think you have some good ideas during the initial part of your probationary period, write them down. After you have gotten to know your supervisor, go to him or her and ask if the organization is receptive to suggestions for change. Be careful not to attack the current system (your supervisor may have proposed it). Instead, suggest that you have been observing and are wondering if you could try something new. This approach is less likely to be viewed as offensive or position you as a know-it-all. If the idea is valid, your supervisor may take immediate action to implement or endorse it.

Respect Others

Your coworkers, vendors, and customers have preferences for what they want, how they want it, and what they like or dislike. Don't try to force your views or preferences on them. This is especially true in today's diverse workplace. Many social and cultural factors contribute to how people act or fail to act. Respect and value these differences. Some typical areas to watch for include:

◆ **Personal space**—*Personal space* refers to how close you stand or sit when communicating. Each culture has acceptable standards of distance between individuals. Violating these distances intentionally or unintentionally can damage relationships and lead to emotional reactions.

**Typical Personal Space Preferences
Observed in the United States**

- Intimate Distance (0 to 18 inches). Normally reserved for close family or intimate relationships.

- Personal Distance (18 inches to 4 feet). Typically reserved for business associates and close friends.

- Work/Social Distance (4 to 12 feet). Maintained at casual business functions or events and during business transactions.

- Public Distance (12 or more feet). Typically observed at large gatherings, presentations, or formal functions.

1

◆ **Personal relationships**—Your ability to do your job, get information required, and access the resources you need often depends on the relationships you build with coworkers, customers, and vendors. Keep in mind that people have differing views of what is respectful and what is not. These views are often the result of cultural heritage or background. While the beliefs of others may differ from your own, you should still respect them in order to maintain and strengthen relationships. Take the time to get to know others and their cultural/personal beliefs (see some of the resources at the end of this book).

> **By building strong relationships, you can identify key people while letting them know your own skills, goals, and abilities.**

By building strong relationships, you can identify key people while letting them know your own skills, goals, and abilities. You should choose relationships carefully and attempt to partner with as many different people as possible. But remember, no matter how strong a relationship you build with someone, you are still in your job for a reason: to get results. Don't let any relationships you develop deter you from this.

◆ **Communication style**—People communicate differently. Some are open and encourage verbal and nonverbal interaction while others are more reclusive and have to be drawn into a conversation. Based on behavioral style preferences, people often demonstrate strong behaviors in the area of communication. For example, some people are "touchy-feely" types who do a lot of touching, stand close while talking, use many hand and facial gestures, and generally exude confidence, warmth, and enthusiasm.

On the other hand, some people smile little, use few gestures, make little eye contact, and prefer not to be touched during communication. An important thing for you to realize in the workplace is that with this type of person (or anyone, for that matter) touching is inappropriate and could send the wrong signals. It might even lead to claims of sexual harassment.

♦ Time allocation—Depending on personality style, some people resent interruption or having someone drop in unexpectedly while others enjoy and invite it. Additionally, the time you commit to spend with people sends strong nonverbal messages. For example, if you tell one person that you have a few minutes to meet with him or her, then spend lengthy periods on a regular basis with someone else, the first person may perceive that you view him or her as less important or that you don't like him or her.

Strategies for Success

Take the time to get to know coworkers. Look for cues about their beliefs, values, and preferences; then respect them. If someone does not like something, trying to change their opinion or ignoring their wishes can cause severe relationship problems. Don't forget that during your initial period, you're trying to build a network, not destroy one.

Do whatever it takes to learn your job roles and expectations.

Be Knowledgeable About Your Job

Do whatever it takes to learn your job roles and expectations. Seek to continually upgrade your knowledge and skills.

Strategies for Success

Solicit written information about your job, organization, and industry from your supervisor and coworkers. Volunteer for training opportunities that might be offered through your department or human resources. Take advantage of educational assistance programs (if available) to expand your knowledge, and talk to experienced employees.

◆ **Demonstrate initiative.** The difference between an average employee and one who excels is the desire to advance and to do more than just what the job requires.

Strategies for Success

Volunteer for additional responsibilities and cross-departmental assignments. Ensure that any product or service you provide meets or exceeds requirements. For example, instead of simply providing information requested by a customer, offer suggestions on how to use or analyze it. Also, after a period of time, follow up with that customer to offer additional assistance.

◆ **Exhibit enthusiasm.** Avoid negative-sounding comments that are intended to be funny or lighthearted. Since people don't know you well, these might be misinterpreted. For example, when someone asks, "How are you today?" don't respond, "I'm here," "Only three more days until Friday," or "Is it quitting time yet?" These types of statements may get back to your supervisor, and he or she might feel that you are dissatisfied with the organization or job. Instead, focus on positive aspects and respond with statements such as, "I'm doing great today, thank you," or "It's another great day at (your organization's name)."

Avoid negative-sounding comments that are intended to be funny or lighthearted.

Strategies for Success

Smile, be positive in responding, and project excitement and energy when given or working on an assignment.

◆ **Contribute to goals.** You are expected to reach established performance goals to help the work unit and organization meet broader objectives. This may involve doing more than just your assigned tasks.

Strategies for Success

Take the time to learn what is expected of you and what your work-unit and organization goals are. Next, work with your supervisor to develop strategies to link the two. When working on a project with others, be willing to help out where needed.

◆ **Avoid office politics.** As the "new kid on the block," you should maintain a low profile by listening, observing, and keeping viewpoints and opinions to yourself—at least initially. Be especially careful about being critical of policies, procedures, systems, or management. Once you are "accepted" into the group and have built a support network, you can gradually become more vocal (within reason). Additionally, you should choose your relationships carefully and not get involved with individuals or groups who are "politically sensitive." Some people have a negative reputation due to poor attitude, a lackadaisical approach to work, or because they refuse to follow established policies and procedures. These people should be avoided.

Strategies for Success

Be congenial with coworkers, but don't get pulled into giving viewpoints, especially negative ones, about your job, supervisor, coworkers, or organization. Some people may have an ulterior motive in soliciting your input, and if the responses get passed along, you could have serious problems.

Using a Mentor to Help You Succeed in Your New Job

One of the best ways for you to learn about the organization, establish yourself, and grow professionally is to find a strong mentor to assist you. Look for someone who is established as well as knowledgeable of the organization.

One of the primary purposes of a good mentor is to guide you to key people who can assist you. These people can ease your entry into the organization.

Some organizations have formal mentoring programs in which they match new employees with a seasoned person. In other organizations, informal systems exist where employees volunteer to help one another. Either way, tapping into the system will benefit you in the long run.

If you are hired from outside the organization, a mentor takes on added value. He or she likely has knowledge of the organizational structure, products, services, and key personnel, and may also possess insight on the cultural and political environment. During the initial stages of your new job, such a resource can prove invaluable.

1

> **One of the best ways for you to learn about the organization is to find a strong mentor to assist you.**

Characteristics of a Good Mentor

When looking for a mentor (in an informal system where one is not provided), you should observe and ask questions about the person you're considering, then talk to him or her directly. Ideally, the person you have targeted should be:

- Willing to mentor.

- Knowledgeable of the organization.

- Politically connected.

- Aware of organizational culture.

- Skilled at problem solving.

- Adaptive.

- An excellent communicator.

- Enthusiastic.

- A good coach.

- Charismatic.

- Trustworthy.

- Patient.

- Accessible.

- A risk-taker.

- Self-confident.

- Creative.

Mentoring: A Shared Responsibility

Keep in mind that for a mentoring relationship to be successful, the person being mentored must also play an active role. Mentoring is a shared responsibility. For you to be successfully mentored, you'll need to personally exhibit the following:

◆ Willingness to learn.

◆ Enthusiasm.

◆ Dedication to working with your mentor.

◆ Initiative.

◆ Open communication skills.

◆ Effective feedback skills.

◆ An inquiring mind.

◆ Conceptual ability (to see the big picture relating your job to the organization).

◆ A positive attitude.

◆ Adaptiveness.

◆ Risk-taking ability.

◆ Self-confidence.

If you and your mentor work together consistently, your horizons can be wide open. In the next chapter, we'll talk more about networking and how valuable it can be in addition to mentoring.

Chapter Summary

Your new position offers opportunities and challenges. Getting all the knowledge and tools you need to be successful is important to your success. While the organization and your supervisor will provide much of what is needed, you'll have to ask questions and do your part too. Taking the time to plan and think ahead as well as looking at the possibility on having a mentor can do much in ensuring your own success.

Self-Check: Chapter 1 Review

Indicate True or False for each of the following statements below. Suggested answers appear on page 76.

1

1. True or False?
   One question you should ask your supervisor is what are his or her expectations of you.

2. True or False?
   Being punctual isn't crucial in some organizations.

3. True or False?
   The way you dress is not important as long as your clothes are clean and in good taste.

4. True or False?
   If you immediately see an opportunity to improve a system after you start your new job, you should push for the change.

5. True or False?
   Continually seeking to improve knowledge and skills can lead to higher levels of success.

6. True or False?
   Your verbal responses to others don't affect their view of your enthusiasm level.

7. True or False?
   One of the primary purposes of a good mentor is to guide you to key people who can assist you.

8. True or False?
   When selecting a mentor, you should observe, ask questions about the person being considered, and talk directly to him or her.

Chapter *Two*

Fitting In and Building Your Network

Chapter Objectives

▶ Use a personal network to succeed in your new job.

▶ Begin to develop effective people skills.

▶ Build trust with your supervisor and coworkers.

▶ Gain better cooperation from others.

Moving into an unknown or new work environment takes a certain amount of confidence and ability, especially if you are new to the organization or work-unit and don't know anyone. To ease the transition and quickly get yourself moving toward job success, you'll need a strong personal and professional network of support. Building or expanding this network can be challenging but can also be easy and fun, depending on your level of enthusiasm and desire.

What Is a Network?

While developing a mentoring relationship such as we discussed in the last chapter is important, having a personal and/or professional network of many people is also crucial for success. Such a network is made up of friends, peers, vendors, customers, or other professionals. Having such connections can mean the difference between your success and failure. From your network, you can obtain the resources you need to gain information, products, or services.

The key to building an effective networking relationship is to remember that in a network, people *share* ideas and information. If you only call upon people to gain something and never take the time to give back information, ideas, or opinions, resentment and a breakdown of the network may result.

Remember that in a network, people *share* ideas and information.

But in a new work environment, many people feel they don't know anyone to contact for information or assistance. This can lead to frustration, inability to function effectively, and, ultimately, failure. According to Fisher and Vilas,[1] effective networks are crucial to business success. Their research found the following:

- A referral generates 80 percent more results than a cold call.

- Approximately 20 percent of all jobs are found through networking.

- Most people you meet have at least 250 contacts.

- Anyone you might want to meet or contact is only four or five people away from you (because each person you contact knows other people, who in turn have contacts, and so on).

Strategies for Success

Take the time to get to know something about coworkers, friends, and people you meet. Find out what and who they know, then catalog that information for future use. Don't be hesitant to call upon these people if needed. Doing so helps maintain contact and strengthens relationships.

[1] Fisher, D. & Vilas, S., *Power Networking: 55 Secrets for Personal and Professional Success,* p. 16, Mountain Harbor Publications, Austin, TX, 1992.

Building Networking Skills

Learning to meet and communicate with others can be intimidating, especially if you're an "outsider" in a new organization. Here are some basic networking tips.

Learn the Value of Small Talk

The term *small talk* has a negative meaning to some and intimidates others. In fact, it simply involves smiling, saying "hello," asking a few questions, listening, and responding positively to the comments of others.

Introduce Yourself Confidently

When you meet people, smile, shake hands firmly, and speak clearly and concisely as you "sell yourself." Then, ask questions about them, what they do, or similar topics—and listen to their responses.

Strategies for Success

Develop a short 30-second or less "advertisement" about yourself to use when meeting new people. Include your name, title, and department (if applicable), and a brief description of what you do (your expertise). The latter should be some task or skill you feel you do well. Longer introductions could sound self-centered and bore people.

Recognize Your Strengths

By knowing what you do or know well, you are able to project enthusiasm when speaking about yourself. You will also be able to easily expand with information on a skill or your knowledge, if asked.

> By knowing what you do or know well, you are able to project enthusiasm when speaking about yourself.

Strategies for Success

Make a list of things you feel you know or do well related to your profession. Once you have your list, develop your 30-second advertisement.

Manage Your Network Resources

A true network is made up of people with whom you maintain regular contact. When you find someone who may be a potential future resource, put extra effort into remembering that person and maintaining contact. To do this, you may want to develop and maintain a system for tracking people. This might be an information card file system, a collection of business cards you have gathered, or PC software specifically designed for contact management.

2

Strategies for Success

When collecting business cards, note bits of information on the back for future reference—date/location met, other people that person knows, who introduced you, and any pertinent information he or she provides (possibly about family members or hobbies). This type of data is great when you next contact him or her because you can repeat bits of information. The person will be flattered and impressed because you "remembered." Doing this can strengthen the relationship.

Be Visible

Allow people to gain access to you in order to expand your network. Also, let people see that you are interested in getting to know them.

Instead of staying locked away in your work area, take opportunities to get out to meet others. Take breaks and eat lunch with coworkers. When attending training sessions, avoid going back to your work area to answer phone messages or "check in." Instead, talk with other attendees.

Take opportunities to get out to meet others.

Take a Moment

Many times, people don't feel what they do is important. The result is that when asked what they do, they provide nondescriptive, almost boring responses which don't encourage follow-up dialogue. Here are some typical occupations, along with common answers and creative alternatives that might stimulate follow-up questions from others.

Occupation	Typical Response	Creative Alternative
Accountant	"I maintain payroll ledgers."	"I ensure everyone gets paid."
Trainer	"I teach classes on . . ."	"I prepare employees for tomorrow's challenges."
Supervisor	"I supervise a staff of . . ."	"I provide an environment for employee success."
Salesperson	"I sell . . ."	"I assist people in making decisions that help them."

Now develop your own alternative.

(Your title) _____   _____

_____

Use your creative alternative next time you're introduced and notice the response.

Getting People to Trust You

As you settle into your job or position, you'll meet many new people. These people will likely be cordial and helpful, but they will not initially depend on you or trust you. This is because you have not yet demonstrated your intentions or abilities. To help encourage better cooperation and foster bonding, try the following:

2

Make Time to Share Information

Once you're seen as a real person, as opposed to someone occupying a position, people normally start to warm up to you.

Show Concern

Demonstrate that you are willing to help others by lending a hand when possible or empathizing with them where appropriate.

Demonstrate
that you are
willing to help
others by
lending a hand
when possible.

Strategies for Success

If you have the time, knowledge, or resources, assist coworkers who are trying to meet a deadline or are performing a task they are not fully qualified for or capable of. This will show that you are concerned about their welfare and success, and they are likely to return the favor in the future.

Be a Team Player

Immediately set about demonstrating that you want to be part of the work-unit. This can be shown through active participation in planning meetings and projects, working with, rather than against, the efforts of others, sharing information and resources freely, supporting and defending the team and its members, and generally exhibiting an "all for one, one for all" attitude daily. Also, participation in on- and off-the-job activities is helpful in reinforcing your inclusive attitude.

Listen, ask questions, show enthusiasm, communicate on a one-on-one level, and don't try to have all the answers.

Strategies for Success

Volunteer to work on group projects and committees, attend after-work gatherings, participate in work-unit brainstorming or problem solving, or offer to assist when needed.

Attributes of an Effective Team Player

Being accepted as a member of the team and performing your roles appropriately in your new work environment requires you to do the following:

Understand your role(s) and those of your coworkers

- Thoroughly understand your role(s) and those of your coworkers.

- Meet your goals.

- Take ownership for tasks, problems, customers, or other situations, whether they are part of your normal job responsibilities or not.

- Pitch in to help solve problems.

- Avoid situations that produce conflict.

- Take a positive "can-do" approach in every work-related activity in which you are involved.

- Demonstrate commitment to supporting departmental goals and objectives.

- Avoid unwarranted complaining. Instead of being part of the problem, become part of the solution by making recommendations for improvement and working to increase quality and quantity output.

- Strive to reduce conflict since it leads to a breakdown in relationships with others, as well as a decrease in productivity and efficiency.

Demonstrate Your Abilities

Your supervisor probably knows your abilities and knowledge levels since he or she interviewed and hired you. On the other hand, coworkers know little or nothing about you. You must sometimes "prove" your worth, especially in a situation in which you were hired from outside the work-unit over an internal candidate. This should not be interpreted to mean that you have to "show off" your talents.

2

Strategies for Success

Verbally communicate your abilities without bragging. Then demonstrate what you know or can do on a regular basis. Whatever you do, ensure that it is done with enthusiasm and to the best of your ability.

Admit Mistakes

Everyone makes errors. The key is to learn from your mistakes and not repeat them. Additionally, if they impact others, apologize and make restitution, if necessary.

Strategies for Success

Acknowledge errors and solicit ideas for correction or improvement. This helps show that you're human, and it can help develop rapport with others while demonstrating that you value their opinions.

Be Consistent and Fair

This is especially important if you are in a supervisory position. By acting in a consistent manner and treating everyone equally, you let people know you are dependable and help them feel comfortable with you. One way to do this in a supervisory or leadership position is to present ideas to others and solicit input, then allow equal access and involvement. For non-supervisors, giving equal attention and spreading your time evenly among others can help send a nonverbal message that you treat everyone as equally important.

> By acting in a consistent manner and treating everyone equally, you let people know you are dependable.

31

Take a Moment

Think of people you have encountered whom you didn't trust. List the reasons for that distrust below. Next, ask others to think about the same question and to add to your list.

_____

_____

_____

_____

_____

_____

Use this list to help prevent making the same mistakes in building trust with others and as a basis for discussion with your coworkers who shared their experiences.

Gaining Cooperation

Your ability to do your job successfully may rest with how well you can get assistance from others. This assistance may come in the form of information, ideas, support for your efforts from others, or actual work assistance or contributions. Much of this cooperation can be tied to trust, but a large percentage is contingent on your ability to communicate your needs and requests to others.

Most people will assist you when asked. Others will want to know, "What is the Added Value And Results For Me (AVARFM)?" Unfortunately, for some people to participate, they must see personal benefit and gain. Follow these guidelines to better gain cooperation from others:

Be Open and Honest

Tell them what you know about the status of projects, goals, issues, or situations. Also, provide timely and honest feedback on issues, concerns, or problems of which you are aware. You were hired to participate, not sit in the background. When giving feedback, keep in mind that it should be objective and provide as many details as possible. Keep it factual and avoid offering opinions unless they are solicited.

2

Your ability to do your job successfully may rest with how well you can get assistance from others.

Strategies for Success

Upon entering into a new team, project, or work environment, immediately make personal contact with all members of the team. Initiate visits to their work stations or offices, or suggest having lunch or taking a break together. Get to know your coworkers on a professional, and possibly a personal, basis.

When giving feedback, try the following model:

◆ **Describe the behavior or situation observed.** Be as specific as possible and focus on the actions of others or the situation rather than on a person. The latter can cause defensiveness, hostility, and damage to relationships (especially with negative or constructive feedback). An example—"I've noticed that no two employees use the same telephone greeting when answering the phone."

◆ **Explain the impact.** Tell what you feel the impact of the observed behavior is or might be. An example—"By not answering the phone in a standard manner, we send a potential message to the customer that we are unprofessional or untrained."

◆ **Describe your feelings.** Tell how you feel about the situation. An example—"I feel that unless we standardize our approach to answering the phone, we might lose customers in the future."

◆ **Solicit input.** Something as simple as a question concerning whether the other person agrees or disagrees can help you determine where he stands and if he correctly heard and interpreted your message meaning. For example—"How do you feel about this?"

◆ **Offer suggestions.** If appropriate, offer ideas for improvement. For example—"I recommend that we consider a telephone courtesy training program for all employees."

◆ **Reaffirm value.** You don't want to be too critical of others; they might take offense. An example—"The manner in which we currently do business obviously works. By adding this new dimension to telephone service, we can potentially increase effectiveness even more."

Listen

When discussing the issue or project with others, take the time to listen for their responses, ideas, reasoning, or concerns.

Strategies for Success

Consciously work toward improving listening skills by using some of the recommendations found in Chapter 3. Keep in mind that as the "newcomer," you want to project a positive image of being a team player and wanting to fit in. Taking time to listen, ask questions, and act upon suggestions will do much to accomplish this.

Do What You Say You're Going to Do

Follow-through on commitments is crucial in developing and maintaining strong trust levels and relationships with others. Too often people will agree to do something without giving thought to the realistic possibilities that they might not have the time, knowledge, skills, or resources to accomplish it. Plan your time well and only commit to things you're sure that you can or will handle.

Be Responsive

When you get a request for information or assistance, even if you can't comply, respond immediately or within 24 hours. If you are not available, make referrals when you know of another resource.

Strategies for Success

Start establishing a reputation for dependability as soon as you begin your new job. Return all phone calls in a timely manner (ideally within 24 hours), arrive on time for work, attend meetings when needed, complete assignments on time, and let others know that you are willing to assist them.

Use a Win-Win Style of Negotiating

If you disagree or are unable to comply with someone, be willing to discuss alternatives or search for other options. Don't simply reject someone's offer or advice and let the issue drop. Strive to establish a win-win situation in which both parties can walk away satisfied that at least part of their needs were met.

Chapter Summary

Moving into a new environment can be a challenging and unique opportunity for growth. It all depends on the way you view the situation and what you make of it. Your best opportunity for success will rest in your ability to quickly meet people, build a network, and integrate yourself into the organizational culture.

Self-Check: Chapter 2 Review

Indicate True or False for each of the statements below.
Suggested answers appear on page 76.

1. True or False?
   A network is made up of peers, vendors, customers, or other professionals.

2. True or False?
   Small talk starts when you say "hello."

3. True or False?
   Taking the time to provide a detailed personal introduction is important when meeting new people.

4. True or False?
   Showing or expressing concern could send a message that you are being nosy or intrusive.

5. True or False?
   Being a team player goes a long way in building trust.

6. True or False?
   If you are hired or promoted over an internal candidate, coworkers will assume you were the best candidate.

7. True or False?
   One way to build trust is to open up and share easily with others.

8. True or False?
   Listening is a key element in gaining cooperation from others.

9. True or False?
   Showing others what they will gain helps get their cooperation in helping you.

2

Chapter *Three*

Communicating in Your New Role and Beyond

Chapter Objectives

▶ Explain the importance of two-way communication in the workplace.

▶ Recognize and use various questioning techniques in interpersonal communication.

▶ Respond better to questions directed to you.

▶ Avoid factors which inhibit your access to effective communication.

▶ Effectively give and receive feedback.

Your first day or week on the job is no time to be timid or reluctant to ask questions.

Your supervisor and organization have initial responsibility for providing you with information that will help you succeed on the job. However, you also have to take the initiative to ask for data and information you feel you need, then listen to the answers. It is during your orientation period that your supervisor is observing your performance and making assessments about you. During the probationary period, people will expect a few errors or omissions from you. Following this initial period, the organization is less likely to forgive errors or omissions because you didn't know something and failed to ask questions.

Communicating Effectively

For effective two-way communication to occur, each person must assume specific roles in a conversation. The two roles—sender and receiver—must be fulfilled appropriately, otherwise a breakdown in message delivery and/or reception can occur. From your perspective as a new employee and message-sender, you should consider numerous factors before starting your message delivery. The following factors must be considered as you "encode" your message for your receiver.

3

- ◆ Physical ability of receiver (Does the person have a hearing loss?)

- ◆ Location of message delivery (Is it noisy or heavily trafficked?)

- ◆ Time and place of delivery (Does the receiver have time to actively listen and is the information of appropriate nature for the location?)

- ◆ Educational/experience background (Does the receiver have the knowledge base to understand your message content?)

- ◆ Language ability (Does the receiver of your message speak or understand the words you use?)

Too often, message-senders inadvertently project a negative image or alienate people by the way they phrase comments, questions, or responses.

Too often, message-senders inadvertently project a negative image or alienate people by the way they phrase comments, questions, or responses. When this happens, communication effectiveness is decreased, and relationships can be damaged.

Take a Moment

The following is a series of negative words or potentially offensive phrases to avoid. After reading each, write your reaction or perceived reaction, then develop an alternate way of positively stating the comment. Possible answers are on page 76.

Avoid These	Possible Interpretation	Possible Alternative
"You must . . ."	_____	_____
"You should . . ."	_____	_____
"You have to . . ."	_____	_____
"I need you to . . ."	_____	_____
"But . . ."	_____	_____
"It's not my job."	_____	_____
"I can't . . ."	_____	_____
"You can't . . ."	_____	_____
"Policy says . . ."	_____	_____
"They require . . ."	_____	_____
"You should/ Why don't you . . ."	_____	_____
"I'll try . . ."	_____	_____

The Art of Questioning

Gaining information is not difficult if you go about it in a logical, well-thought-out manner. The cliché of "you sometimes get what you ask for" certainly applies on the job. If you ask the right questions of the right people, you're likely to get more of what you need to be effective. On the other hand, if you're reluctant to solicit information or ask questions incorrectly, you'll fail to get the answers you want or need to be successful. There are a variety of questions which you might use. Some are more effective than others. Additionally, the way you word your question(s)—voice quality (rate of speech, tone, volume, and pitch), when and where you ask the question(s), and the nonverbal signals you send (stance, facial expression, and gestures)—will all affect the manner in which a person receives the questions and responds.

3

Generally, all questions fall into the categories of open-ended or closed-ended questions.

Open-Ended Questions

Open-ended questions cannot typically be answered with yes or no and are effective for a variety of purposes. They often start with what, how, and why, and they are excellent for encouraging lengthy descriptions of experiences, opinions, instructions, anecdotes, or any topic. Additionally, open-ended questions are good for encouraging people to think and open up with information or ask their own questions. The latter helps continue the conversation. Finally, open-ended questions can be classified as either *general* or *specific.*

♦ **General questions**—With this type of question, you lose control of the discussion and don't know where or how far the listener will go in providing information.

■ Example:
"How have you handled that situation in the past?"

In this example, the person answering may simply say, "I've never had to deal with the situation", or he or she might list dozens of examples and suggestions while adding excessive or unrelated topic information.

♦ **Specific questions**—Specific questions are best for controlling a conversation while obtaining the information you need. Unlike the general question, this type can get you useful information while possibly preventing the listener from rambling. Specific questions may also be worded as assumptive questions in that they presume that the listener will provide the response you're looking for and not simply say "yes" or "no."

■ Example:
"Could you please give me one example of how you've handled that situation in the past?"

In this example, you've allowed the person to open up and share knowledge but have set boundaries on what data or information you're expecting. This type question is useful when time is limited.

Strategies for Success

Before asking any question, determine what information you need. Also, consider the personality type of the person you are dealing with. Some people tend to be more responsive, while others tend to be abrupt or answer with one-syllable replies. Structure questions to address the person's style. For example, to keep a talkative person in check and control the conversation, you might ask more closed-ended questions. For a quiet person, do just the opposite.

While open-ended questions are great for allowing others to share a lot of information, they also lengthen the conversation. There may be times when you simply want a quick piece of information or data or a short response. For these times, you can use the second category of questions known as "closed-ended."

Closed-Ended Questions

Closed-ended questions are effective for getting specific, brief responses. This type of question is good for accomplishing the following:

3

◆ **Controlling the conversation.**

   ■ "Let me ask you a few questions. How long have you worked here? Do you enjoy your job?"

◆ **Saving time.**

   ■ "I've only got a few minutes to get this report to the boss. Can you answer a quick question? Are we going to recommend that new product?"

◆ **Getting quick, one-syllable, or specific responses.**

   ■ "What time is the meeting today?"
      "How long have we carried this product?"
      "Were sales up or down for this product last quarter?"
      "How many different models do we offer?"

◆ **Verifying previously disclosed information for accuracy.**

   ■ "Didn't you say earlier that . . . ?"
      "If I heard you correctly, the Johnson account will result in a 25 percent increase in revenue. Is that correct?"
      "Do I have the information correct?"

◆ **Gaining commitment to an idea, concept, position, or decision.**

   ■ "Does that sound like a logical approach?
      "So, do you think we should proceed as planned?"

◆ Transitioning to a new topic.

■ "Okay, now that we agree on that, can we discuss where we will get the resources needed for this project?"

You should be cautious not to use too many closed-ended questions in a conversation. Excessive use limits the input from others and causes you to do most of the talking. Either can be disastrous when you are trying to build relationships or form new workplace partnerships.

Take a Moment

Since open-ended questions are so valuable for getting people to open up and share valuable information you'll need to get started in your job, spend a little time practicing the development of open-ended questions. Look at each of the following closed-ended examples and convert them to open questions so that you can gain the information needed without changing the focus of the question.
Possible answers are on page 77.

Closed-ended	Open-ended
Do you know how to do . . . ?	What is the best way to do . . . ?
Do I have to do it that way?	_____
Are there other resources available?	_____
Has this been tried before?	_____
Did I do it correctly?	_____
Am I supposed to work alone?	_____
Do I need to get approval before I . . . ?	_____
Others	_____
	_____

Avoiding Communication Turn-Offs

You have probably seen or heard of things that people do which cause others to avoid them. If you were to act similarly in your new workplace environment, your behavior could cause serious communication problems. To prevent making this type of mistake, take a look at the following turn-offs to relationships or communication errors.

◆ **Trying too hard**—Some people try so hard to fit in that they push away those whom they are trying to impress or influence. To avoid this, be yourself. Take the time to smile, listen, and converse with coworkers. Make suggestions, participate in group settings, and maintain an open, friendly manner without pushing into groups or conversations.

◆ **Bragging**—If you have accomplishments of which you are proud, you can make them known without always bringing them up (e.g., distribute a brief biography when you join the team or hang wall plaques/certificates). If people are interested, they will likely ask questions.

◆ **Being a nuisance**—It is all right to call occasionally on someone or drop off information, but repeatedly doing so without invitation can irritate or alienate.

◆ **Giving regular unsolicited advice**—If you feel that you have valuable experiences, information, or insights from which others could benefit, offer, "Say, I've got some information on that. Would you like to see it?"

Based on the other person's response, give him or her the information or let the matter drop, especially if the person seems aversive or noncommittal. He or she could be trying to say "no thanks" without being rude.

3

Some people try so hard to fit in that they push away those whom they are trying to impress or influence.

Listening is a
key commun-
ication skill.

◆ **Displaying biases or prejudices**—There is no place in today's business environment (in any industry) for jokes, remarks, actions, or materials that are discriminatory or offensive to any person or group. This includes issues related to race, sex, gender, religion, age, national/cultural origin, medical conditions, personal attributes, or any other area. In a society where diversity issues are so prominent and important, acting inappropriately or in a bigoted manner could mean disaster for your career opportunities and lead to personal legal liability as well.

Listening for Success

During your initial or probationary period on the job, most of your time will be spent gathering information. You'll be learning about your supervisor's expectations, job requirements, the organization, and a variety of other topics. You'll gather much of this information through listening.

According to Barbara Zarna,[2] 10 percent of new employees don't successfully make it through their probationary period. Many of the reasons for their failure can be directly related to their communication ability. Listening is a key communication skill. Research has shown that most adults listen at only about a 25 percent efficiency rate. That means that they miss 75 percent of what is said to them! Bottom line—if you fail to listen, you don't succeed.

[2] Zarna, B., *The Job Search: Your Guide to Success,* pg 39, Richard D. Irwin, Burr Ridge, IL, 1994.

Recognizing Poor Listening

Pay attention to signals given by others which might indicate that they perceive that you are not listening effectively. Some telltale signs are actions such as the following:

◆ Others have to repeat information for you.

◆ You find yourself leaving a conversation or meeting and not knowing details discussed.

◆ People bypass you to go to others to discuss things.

◆ Coworkers rarely share personal information or experiences with you.

◆ You never seem to get information others have.

◆ You are the last to know about something.

◆ Deadlines sneak up on you.

◆ You hear statements such as:
  • "Are you listening to me?"
  • "You aren't listening."
  • "Did you hear what I just said?"

Strategies for Success

To ensure that you are practicing active listening skills, go into the listening situation in the following manner.
• Stop other activities.
• Transfer phone calls or use an answering machine, if possible.
• Get away from distracting things or people.
• Mentally prepare to listen.
• Face the person, or, if on the telephone, face a wall (to avoid desktop distractions).
• Ask for clarification or feedback when appropriate.

Take a Moment

Think about a time when you had difficulty dealing with someone because that person was not listening effectively. Perhaps you were at a restaurant, supermarket, automobile repair shop, laundry, or your home.

What happened to make you believe that the person wasn't listening?

_____

How did you feel about that person's inattention?

_____

What was the outcome of the encounter?

_____

What can you do to ensure you don't copy the negative behavior?

_____

Chapter Summary

Without refining your ability to communicate with others, you stand a chance of either being less successful or failing in your efforts on your new job. With the Number 1 problem area in organizations revolving around poor interpersonal communications, you cannot afford to be inhibited in your efforts due to poor listening, verbal, or nonverbal communication skills. Take the time to honestly assess your strengths and areas for improvement related to interpersonal communication, then invest the time and effort to make necessary improvements. No matter how effective you believe you are, there is always room for improvement.

Self-Check: Chapter 3 Review

Indicate True or False for each of the following statements. Suggested answers appear on page 78.

1. True or False?
   Most adults listen at about a 75 percent efficiency rate.

2. True or False?
   Listening is a learned behavior.

3. True or False?
   Because of communication-related issues, 10 percent of all new employees don't make it through their employment probation period.

4. True or False?
   Your supervisor and organization has the initial responsibility for providing you with job-related information.

5. True or False?
   Questions which start with what, how, and why are typically closed-ended.

6. True or False?
   Open-ended questions are good for gaining a lot of information.

7. True or False?
   Open-ended questions can be classified as either specific or general.

8. True or False?
   Questions that cannot be answered with short or one-syllable answers are called closed-ended.

9. True or False?
   When first meeting someone, you should use open-ended questions to learn more about them.

10. True or False?
    If you never seem to get information others have, you may not be listening effectively.

Chapter *Four*

Preparing for the Unexpected

Chapter Objectives

▶ Prepare yourself for some of the unexpected occurrences you might encounter during the initial job transition period.

▶ Handle a variety of common challenges faced by new employees.

In an ideal world, you would be able to select the organization for which you want to work, apply and be hired for the job of your choice, meet your new boss and coworkers, then smoothly slip into your new position and live happily ever after. Unfortunately, this isn't always the case. How you deal with problems or unexpected events is often dependent upon how well you anticipate and prepare.

Why Things Go Wrong

Many supervisors have the best intentions when dealing with their employees. They probably realize that their role is to provide a positive, supportive work environment where employees can do their job to the best of their abilities. Additionally, most supervisors understand the need for ongoing coaching and support which allows employee knowledge to grow while they develop new job skills. This all sounds good in theory—but then there's reality! Reality sometimes has a way of forcing changes in goals and priorities as events unfurl for supervisors and employees.

Many things can prevent supervisors from carrying out their goals of communicating information and providing timely, specific performance feedback to employees. As a result, you may have to be creative in gathering job-related information.

Playing "What If . . ."

Take a look at the following situations and think of how you might handle them if they happened to you.

What If . . .

. . . you interviewed for a new job, received an acceptance letter from the organization congratulating and welcoming you and asking you to report on a specific date to work? Excitedly, you show up on your first day to find that your supervisor has to be out of the office for your first three or four days.

What would you do? _____

_____

4

Obviously, this is not the way for your new supervisor to make a positive first impression or help you quickly get into the mainstream of your new job. The nonverbal message could be that you're not very important. But don't jump to conclusions. There may be extenuating circumstances, such as a personal or operational emergency. Besides, your immediate attention should be on how you can successfully get going in your new job. Here are some possible strategies you might use.

Your immediate attention should be on how you can successfully get going in your new job.

◆ Report to your department and, if your supervisor has one, meet his or her secretary. Ask if directions were left for you and for any suggestions the secretary may have. Possibly request that he or she contact the supervisor for instructions/guidance.

◆ Report to your department and try to identify a senior employee, possibly an assistant to the supervisor or a peer coach. Ask for advice or guidance.

◆ Report to Human Resources/Personnel, explain the situation, and ask for guidance.

◆ As a last resort, contact your supervisor's boss and introduce yourself. Ask for guidance. The supervisor may have forgotten you were starting and didn't plan for your arrival. But be careful. Bringing such an oversight to the boss's attention could cause friction between you and your supervisor later.

What If . . .

. . . during your first week of work, your supervisor assigns you a very important project with unrealistic completion deadlines, ignoring the fact that you don't feel you've had time to adjust to your new environment and responsibilities?

What would you do? _____

_____

Begin by considering potential causes for such deadlines or pressure. Maybe your boss is under the impression that you possess adequate time, knowldege, or experience to handle the assignment. Or perhaps, he or she is being pressured from above. In any event, the following approaches may help.

◆ Request to meet with your boss and provide open, honest feedback about your feelings and concerns. Offer any alternatives you can think of, solicit options from him or her, and ask for assistance in planning to meet the deadline(s).

◆ Look to others whom you've met within the organization for advice and guidance.

◆ Meet with your supervisor to determine if other, more experienced employees could work with you on the project.

◆ Research files and talk to coworkers to determine if similar projects have been successfully completed before. If so, model your efforts after those projects.

What If . . .

. . . you start your new job, and within the first week an immediate family member becomes seriously ill and is hospitalized?

How would you handle the situation? _____

_____

There is no good time for such an event to occur, but particularly in a new job situation, such timing would not be advantageous. However, as inconvenient or untimely as such an occurrence would be for your supervisor or organization, most people would empathize with your need to care for your family. In fact, within reason, many organizations have written value or belief statements which stress "commitment to employees." Therefore, within reason, you can expect assistance in dealing with the situation. The following are suggestions you may want to consider.

◆ Go to your supervisor immediately and inform him or her of the situation, explain the impact on you (e.g., you need time off to care for a sick family member), and ask for assistance.

◆ Check with your Human Resources/Personnel department to determine if any policies or laws are in place to assist you in such instances. Also, if applicable, determine what medical benefits might apply.

◆ As soon as you determine the seriousness of the situation, update your supervisor and then keep him or her advised as things change.

What If . . .

. . . you start your new position and shortly thereafter realize that the job you have is not the one you thought you were taking, in regard to actual tasks and responsibilities?

What would you do? _____

_____

Occasionally, due to the excitement of getting a job, some people fail to adequately investigate what they'll be doing. This could be due to poor listening or failing to ask the right questions during an employment interview. Another possibility is that the interviewer didn't adequately screen the applicant's background, listen to the applicant, or ask the right questions to determine how the applicant's qualifications matched the job requirements.

In any case, you need to address the issue quickly. The longer you are in the position, the more you'll be expected to do. You could become unhappy, let your performance drop, and/or face disciplinary action.

Some options in this situation include the following:

♦ If you feel you can gain the necessary skills rather quickly, you might set out to read about or practice these skills while you continue in the position.

♦ Go to your supervisor, honestly discuss the situation, and jointly make a decision on what's best for you and the organization.

♦ Identify an experienced peer, and solicit his or her assistance as a coach to help you learn what's necessary.

What If . . .

. . . shortly after starting your new job, you realize that you have a strong dislike for or a personality difference with your supervisor?

What would you do? _____

_____

Differing values, beliefs, and style preferences can sometimes lead to conflict.

People don't always get along with each other. Differing values, beliefs, and style preferences can sometimes lead to conflict or at least to a very uncomfortable relationship. If this occurs with your boss, you need to take steps to correct the situation immediately. You depend on your supervisor for guidance, support, and assistance. He or she is also responsible for reporting on your performance and could impact your career or opportunities for financial reward.

Typically, what happens when a clash of personalities occurs is that one or both people are either not communicating or are unwilling to bend their beliefs and compromise. Since your supervisor is in a position of authority and power, it is to your advantage to comply with his or her wishes (within moral, legal, and ethical limitations) and to work toward strengthening the relationship. Remember, you can't change others, but you can change yourself. Your other option might be to leave the organization or department, depending on the situation.

You can't change others, but you can change yourself.

Other possibilities include the following:

◆ Sit down with an experienced, knowledgeable person whom you trust. Discuss the situation with him or her and ask for advice before taking any action. Remember, this person should have real-world business experience. Your best friend may make you feel good by empathizing with you but probably won't be able to offer valid suggestions.

◆ Research personality styles and consider taking a behavioral styles self-assessment test to determine your own preferences. By understanding yourself, you can better understand others and possibly work more effectively with them. There are many possible sources for self-assessments.[3]

◆ Evaluate your communication style and determine how you can improve. Admit shortcomings in your listening, verbal, and nonverbal skills, and work toward improvement. There are many excellent courses, books, audiotapes, and videotapes available that can help.

◆ Set up a meeting with your supervisor and, in a non-confrontational manner, discuss your feelings. Solicit his or her assistance in helping the two of you build a stronger relationship. Remember, if you never discuss the issue, you can't find the best solution.

◆ Contact your organization's Employee Assistance Program counselors (if this program is available). An EAP is a non-threatening and confidential resource.

[3] One source is Creative Presentation Resources™, Casselberry, FL, (800) 308-0399.

♦ As a last resort, go to your supervisor's boss or to Human Resources/Personnel and ask for assistance.

Strategies for Success

Remember, you can change yourself, but not others. Also, it may be only your perception that the relationship is not working. Because of his or her behavioral style or for other reasons, your supervisor may not share your perception.

What If . . .

. . . you realize that you have a strong dislike or personality difference with a coworker?

What would you do? _____

_____

As in the previous situation, you need to address the issue immediately. As discussed earlier in the book, you are new and need to fit into the team. Don't forget, your coworker is established and probably has a support network and friends whom he or she might influence against you. The earlier you address the issue in a nonconfrontational manner, the better off you'll be. In addition to the strategies mentioned for the last situation, try the following:

The earlier you address a personality conflict, the better off you'll be.

♦ Set up an informal meeeting (possibly lunch outside the building) to discuss how the two of you can better support each other. Be candid about your feelings and concerns, and request your coworker's perceptions or feedback on how he or she feels the relationship is going.

♦ If there are actions or inactions on the coworker's part which impede your ability to meet job standards or requirements, and he or she is unwilling to change, go to your supervisor immediately. Ultimately, you will be held responsible for your performance, not your coworker's.

What If . . .

. . . after you start your new job, you discover that you're required to perform tasks but don't have the required materials, tools, or training needed?

What should you do? _____

_____

Here are some possible options to resolve this issue:

◆ Check with coworkers performing similar jobs to determine their sources for materials, tools, and equipment.

◆ Meet with your supervisor to determine what resources are available for receiving training or instruction (e.g., peer coaches, on-the-job training, formal organizational training programs, outside seminars).

◆ Look for manuals, books, videos, audiotapes, or other information that will allow you to train yourself.

What If . . .

. . . within your first week of employment, you learn that there have been numerous people in your position during the past six months, all of whom have resigned?

What action should you take? _____

_____

Rather than jumping to conclusions, you may want to try one or more of the following actions.

◆ Ask your boss for his or her perspective.

◆ Ask coworkers what they know of the turnover (e.g., reasons, causes).

4

◆ Don't get too concerned about the situation. If you like the job, people, and environment, make the most of your opportunities. If your job is an entry-level or support position, chances are some people may have used it as an entry point into the organization and then may have moved on.

What If . . .

. . . you find that your job requires you to work with customers, coworkers, or vendors who are different from you (e.g., language, race, disabilities, culture)?

What would you do? _____

_____

> **The key to your success—on the job as well as off—is to focus on similarities, rather than differences, in people.**

As part of a rapidly changing world, you are likely to encounter diversity in all aspects of your life. The key to your success—on the job as well as off—is to focus on similarities, rather than differences, in people. By better understanding the needs of others and making an effort to work with them, you can improve relationships. Try the following to help reduce your tensions and anxieties.

◆ Review some of the resources on communication and relationships listed at the end of this book.

◆ Take the time to listen effectively, then respond appropriately to others.

◆ Gain additional knowledge related to different cultures, people with disabilities, languages, races, and religions. This can be done by visits to the library, bookstores, seminars, college courses, or regular interaction with a variety of people or groups.

◆ Learn to use effective verbal and nonverbal communication skills.

◆ Make an effort to interact with others who are different in order to better understand their beliefs, needs, and preferences.

What If . . .

. . . shortly after starting your new job, new technology with which you are uncomfortable or unfamiliar is introduced into your organization or job?

What would you do? _____

_____

Technology changes are a common part of today's competitive business environment. Organizations or people reluctant to change are fair targets for failure. Generally, when technology is introduced into an organization, adequate training of employees follows. Even so, you should strive to learn the capabilities and limitations, and if appropriate, the safety features of the new technology, as quickly as possible. The faster you master the equipment, the more proficient and productive you can become. In addition to the training you may receive, consider the following strategies.

4

Strive to learn the capabilities and limitations of new technology as quickly as possible.

- ◆ Read any manuals or materials accompanying the technology.

- ◆ If available, work with someone who is proficient with the technology in order to improve more quickly.

- ◆ Practice, practice, practice. The more you use the technology, the more you will learn and the better you will become with it.

What If . . .

. . . you are assigned tasks you'd rather not do or don't like?

How would you handle the situation? _____

_____

Every job has associated tasks which you may not enjoy or prefer to do. The key to success is to remember that you were hired to do a job. If that job includes, or your supervisor assigns, undesirable tasks, it is your responsibility to accomplish them to the best of your ability. To better handle such tasks, try the following:

◆ Meet with your supervisor in an effort to try to determine the significance of the assigned tasks. Often, seeing what you do in conjunction with the bigger picture helps you realize the importance of your job.

◆ Use positive self-talk to reassure yourself that the task is only a portion of your job and that there are many positive benefits and portions of the job and organization.

◆ Continue to learn about the organization, products and services offered, and opportunities. When another position for which you are qualified becomes available, you can then apply for it.

Chapter Summary

There are many positive aspects to your new job. Spend the time necessary to prepare for your new role(s) and address issues which surface in a professional manner.

No doubt your new job has many positive aspects. Devote the necessary time to prepare for your new role(s), and address issues that surface in a professional manner. Rather than complaining, ignoring a situation, or trying to escape it, look for ways to resolve the issues and get back on track.

Self-Check: Chapter 4 Review

Indicate True or False to the following statements. Answers appear on page 78.

1. True or False?
    Should your supervisor not be in the office the day you begin work, you should immediately contact his or her boss to inform them of the situation.

2. True or False?
    Absence due to illness of a family member during your probationary period could be seen as a poor attitude on your part and might cause disciplinary problems.

3. True or False?
    Generally, when a new employee realizes that his or her job isn't what he or she thought it would be, it is because the interviewer misrepresented it.

4. True or False?
    If you and your supervisor have a personality clash, there is little you can do other than tolerate the situation or leave the organization.

5. True or False?
    One strategy for dealing with a coworker with whom you're having difficulty is to request to meet informally to discuss options.

6. True or False?
    Should you find out that there have been a lot of people in your position before you arrived, you should immediately become concerned.

7. True or False?
    Diversity is commonplace in the global world of today. Learning to appreciate strengths rather than differences is your key to success.

4

Chapter *Five*

Beyond Orientation

Chapter Objectives

▶ Understand your supervisor's and your own responsibility for a successful orientation.

▶ Develop a personal action plan to gain additional information and resources you'll need to succeed.

▶ Set personal goals for your introductory (probation) period.

▶ Recognize how to demonstrate your enthusiasm toward your job.

Many people believe that orientation is where new employees are shown all they'll need to be successful in their new job. However, orientation is only the beginning. Your job-related education begins in earnest once you meet your coworkers, customers, and supervisor. If your supervisor doesn't realize and plan for this reality, you may ultimately fail or at least experience a great degree of frustration. That's the bad news. The good news is that most organizational managers realize the importance of integrating new employees into the system quickly and, as such, your supervisor is probably anxiously awaiting your arrival.

Your Supervisor's Responsibility

Prior to your arrival, your supervisor will likely select a volunteer coworker to act as your peer coach. Or your supervisor may elect to perform the task him or herself. The role of the peer coach will be to act as your mentor. In that capacity, he or she will help ensure that you are able to translate the information offered in your orientation to your new job. The following checklists show information that will be covered by your supervisor, as well as questions you may have of him or her.

Supervisor's Workplace Orientation Checklist

◆ Welcome/introduction to staff

◆ Tour of work area

◆ Discussion of work-unit policies/procedures

◆ Sharing of departmental mission statement/objectives

◆ Discussion of job description

◆ Discussion/review of performance appraisal system/form

◆ Setting of employee performance goals

◆ Tour of building (restrooms, emergency exits, break/lunch areas, reproduction area, mailroom, and other pertinent areas)

◆ Identification of supply location(s)

◆ Tour of customer areas/support departments

◆ Overview of phone etiquette standards/voice mail/fax procedures

◆ Discussion of training schedule (for skill and knowledge development)

◆ Assignment of tasks/projects

5

Possible Questions for Your Supervisor

If your supervisor fails to provide pertinent information that you feel is needed to do your job effectively, you may have to request a meeting and ask some specific questions. The following are general questions that may gain valuable background information. Add others that you feel are important.

◆ What will be my work schedule?

◆ When will my performance be formally evaluated?

◆ Of what specific policies/procedures should I be aware?

◆ What is your style of management?

◆ What is your vision of my role?

◆ What professional development opportunities do I have available?

◆ What do you expect from your employees?

Others _____

_____

_____

_____

Your Responsibilities

In today's global business environment, strategies, products, services, and technologies continue to change. As your organization or department evolves to meet new challenges, your ability to adapt to these changes will determine your level of job success. Depending on how dynamic your coworkers and workplace environment turn out to be, you may have to exhibit a high degree of initiative to obtain what you need to do your job. You cannot expect that everything will automatically be provided to you. Furthermore, you must be prepared to look outside the organization for additional resources and opportunities for growth. The following are some suggestions for future development.

> **You must be prepared to look outside the organization for additional resources and opportunities for growth.**

◆ **Determine necessary knowledge, skills, and aptitudes needed.** After reviewing your job description with your supervisor, you should have a good idea of what is needed to reach effective performance levels. Compare the list identified to your current knowledge and skill levels; then develop a plan for continued growth.

◆ **Target training needs.** Working with your supervisor, establish a performance development plan. As part of this process, request to participate in appropriate specific training programs or developmental activities (e.g., on-the-job training, personal computer-based training, self-study, college/university courses, or professional development seminars).

◆ **Read organizational publications.** If your organization has a newsletter or magazine, or publishes customer literature, get recent copies and review them. Then regularly read these publications as they are developed. This is a quick method for finding out the pulse of the organization, determining key issues, and identifying key personnel.

◆ **Review departmental staff memorandums.** Try to arrange access to any file containing "all staff" type memorandums from the CEO/President and/or your department head. Go back approximately six months to get a feel for the culture and to identify hot issues.

5

◆ **Meet with counterparts.** If your job is such that employees in other departments are doing similar jobs or will interact with you on projects, get to know them. Either set up formal meetings or arrange breaks, lunch, or after-work get togethers.

◆ **Read trade publications.** If there are publications aimed at your occupation or industry, seek them out. Either subscribe or go to the library to access and read them regularly. These publications will provide insights into what other organizations are doing and changes in the industry.

◆ **Join a professional organization.** If there is a local professional organization for your industry, become an active member. Such organizations often provide regular meetings with speakers, publish newsletters, have information banks, and offer opportunities for networking. Don't simply join; actively participate on committees, possibly playing a leadership role. The latter is a great way to let people know who you are and to help build leadership skills which can be transferred to the job.

◆ **Seek new opportunities.** Once you learn and master your basic job responsibilities, seek out other chances to demonstrate your abilities and desire to grow. Your initiative and enthusiasm will not only likely be contagious, but also can lead to future opportunities and advancement.

Take a Moment

Consider your first six months on the job.

What do you want to accomplish?

_____

List anything you perceive to be potential barriers to your success.

_____

_____

What is/are your biggest concern(s)?

_____

What can you do to alleviate the concern(s) you just identified?

_____

_____

Use this information in your discussion with your supervisor and/or peer coach.

5

You may find that you still need or are curious about resources that can help you succeed in your new job. It is up to you to find these additional resources and to take action to gain all the information you can. Use the following plan to help you organize your search for more information.

Personal Action Plan

To better acclimate myself to my new job, I will take the following actions:

Action:	By Date:
Obtain a copy of my job description from my supervisor or Human Resources/Personnel.	_____
Work with my supervisor to prepare a personal development plan.	_____
Obtain the past six copies of organizational publications (i.e., newsletters, customer magazines, hot sheets) for review.	_____
Review departmental memorandums issued within the past six months.	_____
Set up meetings/lunches with peers or counterparts in other departments, as well as vendors and/or customers to develop a network.	_____
Contact the public library to identify and obtain available professional/trade publications applicable to my job.	_____
Contact the American Society for Associations to identify local and national organizations pertinent to my field/job.	_____

Setting Personal Goals

Rather than assuming someone else will guide you, take the initiative to go after what you need to do your job. Continue to grow and look for new opportunities. To accomplish this, you'll need specific, measurable goals. Otherwise, you won't have a projected purpose and won't be able to determine if you've accomplished it.

Goals are generally based on needs or desired outcomes. For example, if you are working on a major project that will ultimately impact your performance appraisal rating, your goal may be to complete the project on or ahead of schedule.

Additional potential goals and associated factors are shown below.

Projected Needs	Ultimate Goal(s)	Actions Required to Attain
Become part of departmental team.	Perform job well.	Get out and meet others.
Get promoted.	Make more money.	Perform at a high level. Continue to improve knowledge and skills.
Gain more knowledge.	Complete college degree.	Check with supervisor or HR to determine educational assistance policy; contact local colleges/universities for schedule.

5

Positive Reinforcement

To become successful at accomplishing your goals, you'll need positive reinforcement. Typically, your organization/supervisor provides this in the form of verbal praise, financial rewards, professional development opportunities, and tangible rewards (i.e., luncheons, certificates/plaques) when you accomplish job-related goals.

You can also reward yourself for accomplishment by giving yourself such things as a break or cup of coffee after you reach a goal of typing a lengthy report, a movie or video for completing a correspondence course on schedule, or a vacation or weekend escape with your spouse, friend, or significant other following a lengthy, important project.

The key is to ensure that the reward is effective in reinforcing your accomplishment. It should follow completion of a specific project or phase and be linked directly to the goal(s).

To determine if the goal is complete, it must be measurable. Traditionally, goals are measured in terms of the following:

◆ Time (i.e., within a certain time frame)

◆ Money (i.e., savings/earnings/costs)

◆ Quality (i.e., degree of effectiveness/percentage of improvement)

◆ Quantity (i.e., number of items completed/produced)

Make your goals attainable, otherwise you'll get disappointed or frustrated, and your performance may suffer.

Take a Moment

Now that you've had a chance to think about your new position, what's expected, and some things to expect, take a few minutes to set some personal goals before you get too far along in your new job.

Projected Needs	Ultimate Goal(s)	Actions Required to Attain
_____	_____	_____
_____	_____	_____
_____	_____	_____
_____	_____	_____
_____	_____	_____

5

Developing the Attitude to Succeed

You may have heard the cliché that being able to succeed is often mind over matter—you don't mind; it doesn't matter! While this sounds like a potential solution, it's not realistic. In fact, your attitude and how much attention you pay to your new work environment is crucial to your success.

So what is attitude? Basically, it's your mental state toward something or someone. It's the way you act, feel, or think. In relation to your new position, it could be very positive because you've taken the time to research the type of job you want and the organization for which you wish to work. On the other hand, it could be lukewarm because you simply accepted "a job" in order to pay your bills. Obviously, the latter is likely to lead to a lack of enthusiasm about the job, your responsibilities, and your employer.

Let's assume you are excited about your new job and examine how your employer might know this. The following are indicators of a "good" attitude that can lead to your success.

Although some points have been covered in earlier chapters, it is important to realize how these elements of a positive attitude relate to your success on the job.

Punctuality and Regular Attendance

Always strive to be at your workplace when you are scheduled to work. Few actions send a message of poor attitude faster than an employee with a tardiness or absenteeism pattern. Calling in to say you're going to be late does not excuse you for being late. People who regularly arrive late, take extended lunch periods and breaks, or simply do not show up as scheduled are due to have disciplinary problems. Common excuses, such as "my car broke down," "the baby-sitter didn't show up," "my alarm didn't go off," or "my kids are sick," may be valid but do not make the problems created by your absence any more acceptable, especially if such excuses are heard regularly.

Solid Productivity

After being properly trained, provided with appropriate equipment/materials, and given time to develop your skills, you will be expected to meet minimum job standards and produce at the same levels as your peers. Consistent failure to do so could lead to trouble.

Strategies for Success

Continually strive to upgrade your skills and knowledge. Be conscious of established standards and work to improve speed, efficiency, and effectiveness.

High Morale

Everyone has run-ins with others or a bad day from time to time. The key to overcoming these difficulties is to not stay focused on a negative incident and allow it to get you down. Realize that such problems are normal, and don't spend time complaining to others. If you develop a reputation as a whiner, you'll set yourself up for loss of friends and a potential collision with your supervisor. Strive to be the person who smiles often and has a good word for others.

Strategies for Success

Practice positive "self-talk." Continually remind yourself of the positives related to your job, benefits, coworkers, organization, and life. Don't dwell on the negatives; they'll only depress you.

Willingness to Help

From time to time, you'll be asked to pitch in to help your boss, coworkers, or others in the organization. If at all possible, take the time to do what you can. This will send a message that you care and are part of the team. Be assured that at some point, your enthusiasm and helpfulness will be rewarded.

Strategies for Success

Take advantage of informal meetings, such as lunch time or breaks, to let your peers and your supervisor know of your strengths and skills and also your willingness to help others in times of need.

5

Enthusiasm

Tackle every new task with zeal. Develop a reputation of "no task is too big or too small" for you to handle. When working with others, vocalize positives instead of negatives. Help others be successful by always setting the example.

Strategies for Success

Volunteer for assignments whenever possible or practical. This shows your willingness to do more than just meet job standards or maintain status quo. It also identifies you as a strong team player.

Chapter Summary

Your level of success will depend to a great extent on how well you and your supervisor coordinate the performance goals that have been established for you. Getting off to a good start, then continuing to solidify your skills and knowledge is crucial. As you prepare to start your new job or begin to settle into it, keep the things you've read in mind. Take the time to go back and review the activities and the key points made. Like anything else in life, your new job will be what you make it.

What's Next?

The next move is yours. After reading the contents of this book, developing a strategy, and reporting to work, you'll be on your way to success!

Good luck!!

Answers to Selected Exercises

Chapter 1

Review (page 23)

1. True	5. True
2. False	6. False
3. False	7. True
4. False	8. True

Chapter 2

Review (page 37)

1. True	6. False
2. True	7. True
3. False	8. True
4. False	9. True
5. True	

Chapter 3

Take a Moment (page 40)

Avoid These	Possible Interpretation	Possible Alternative
"You must . . ."	Very Commanding/ Offensive	"One thing you may want to try/consider . . ."
"You should . . ."	Controlling/Domineering	"Do you think _____ could work?"
"You have to . . ."	Controlling/Domineering	"It would be helpful if you _____. Do you think that's possible?"
"I need you to . . ."	Pressuring	"Would you please help by . . ."
"But . . ."	Forget everything previously said, here's my *real* message	Instead simply deliver your single message

"It's not my job." | Find someone who cares | "Although I don't normally handle that, how may I assist you?"

"I can't . . ." | I don't want to | "What can I do?"

"You can't . . ." | We/I forbid you | "While we're unable to . . . maybe we can . . . "

"Policy says . . ." | We're not willing to adapt or make changes | What we can do is . . . "

"They require . . . " | I don't have the power or authority | "What I can try/do is . . . "

"You should/ Why don't you . . . " | Pushing/Pressuring | "Could we . . . instead?"

"I'll try . . ." | I'm fairly powerless | "I will/can . . ."

Take a Moment (page 44)

Closed-ended	Open-ended
Do you know how to do . . . ?	What is the best way to do . . . ?
Do I have to do it that way?	What are my options for doing it?
Are there other resources available?	What other resources are available?
Has this been tried before?	What approaches have been tried in the past?
Did I do it correctly?	What suggestions do you have for future improvement?
Am I supposed to work alone?	Who else will be working with me?
Do I need to get approval before I . . . ?	What level of authority or decision making do I have?

Review (page 49)

1. True
2. True
3. True
4. True
5. False

6. True
7. True
8. False
9. True
10. True

Chapter 4

Review (page 61)

1. False
2. False
3. False
4. False
5. True

6. False
7. True

Additional Resources

◆ Alessandra, T., *People Smart: Powerful Techniques for Turning Every Encounter into a Mutual Win,* Keynote Publishing, La Jolla, CA, 1992.

◆ Alessandra, T. and Hunsaker, P., *Communicating at Work,* Simon & Schuster, New York, NY, 1993.

◆ Axtell, R.E., *Dos and Taboos Around the World,* John Wiley & Sons, New York, NY, 1990,

◆ Axtell, R.E., *Gestures: Dos & Taboos of Body Language Around the World,* John Wiley & Sons, New York, NY, 1991.

◆ Bolton, R. and Boltin, D.G., *Social Style/Management Style: Developing Productive Work Relationships,* AMACOM, New York, NY, 1984.

◆ Dugger J., *Listen Up: Hear What's Really Being Said,* American Media Publishing, West Des Moines, IA, 1995.

◆ Hilgermann, R.H., *Goal Management at Work,* Richard D. Irwin, Burr Ridge, IL, 1994.

◆ Lewis, D., *The Secret Language of Success: Using Body Language to Get What You Want,* Carroll & Graf Publishers, New York, NY, 1989.

◆ Lucas, R.W., *Customer Service: Skills and Concepts for Business,* Richard D. Irwin, Burr Ridge, IL, 1995.

◆ Lucas, R.W., *Effective Interpersonal Relationships,* Richard D. Irwin, Burr Ridge, IL, 1994.

◆ Matt Yanna, M., *Attitude: The Choice is Yours,* American Media Publishing, West Des Moines, IA, 1996.

◆ Morris, D., *Body Talk: The Meaning of Human Gestures,* Crown Trade Paperbacks, New York, NY, 1994.

◆ Quick, T.L., *Understanding People at Work: A Management Guide to the Behavioral Sciences,* Executive Enterprises, New York, NY, 1976.

● Additional Resources

◆ Shelton, N. and Burton, S., *Assertiveness Skills,* American Media Publishing, West Des Moines, IA, 1995.

◆ Towers, M., *Self-Esteem: The Power to Be Your Best,* American Media Publishing, West Des Moines, IA, 1995.

◆ Vogues, K. and Braund, R., *Understanding How Others Misunderstand You,* Moody Press, Chicago, IL, 1990.

◆ Wolvin, A. and Coakley, C.G., *Listening,* Brown and Benchmark, Madison, WI, 1996.